PYTHON PROGRAMMING BIBLE FOR BEGINNERS 2024

python mastery crash course (Essential Python Skills for Success)

Joe J. Meyer

Table Of Contents

Part 1: Dive into the Python Playground (No Prior Experience Needed!)

In Part 1 of "Python Programming for Beginners 2024: Unleash Your Coding Superpowers!", we will dive headfirst into the Python playground, the place where no prior experience is needed. This part of the route is designed to welcome complete beginners to the world of Python programming and grant a mild introduction to the language.

We will explore the fundamentals of Python, along with its syntax, statistics types, and vital concepts, putting a sturdy foundation for your coding journey. Through interactive workouts and hands-on practice, you will rapidly feel at home in the Python playground and start to free up the thrilling possibilities that coding in Python has to offer. Get ready to embark on this interesting adventure with us as we kickstart your coding journey in Part 1!

Chapter 1: Welcome to Python! - Why Python Rocks and What You Can Build (Spoiler Alert: It's Awesome!)

Welcome to the thrilling world of Python programming! Buckle up and get geared up to unleash your internal creator, because Python is about to take you on an excellent journey. In this chapter, we will delve into the motives why Python is viewed as one of the most cherished programming languages in the world, and discover the large array of matters you can convey to lifestyles with its help.

Why Python Rocks: Unveiling the Magic

Python has earned its popularity as a rockstar language for a multitude of reasons. Here's a closer look at what makes it so special:

- **Beginner-friendly:** Unlike some programming languages that can resemble cryptic puzzles, Python boasts a clear and concise syntax. This means the code you write will look more like natural language, making it easier to understand, learn, and remember.

- **Versatility is unbound:** Python is a proper chameleon, capable of adapting to a vast variety of programming domains. Whether you are developing web applications, statistics science projects, desktop learning algorithms, automation scripts, or even games, Python has the equipment and libraries to make it happen.

- **Readability for the win:** Imagine being in a position to write code that appears almost like simple English! Python's focal point on readability makes it less complicated for you and others to apprehend the logic in the back of your code. This is a main benefit when you need to collaborate with different programmers or revisit your code after some time.

- **Free and open-source:** Python is free to use and modify, thanks to its open-source nature. This opens doors for a vibrant neighborhood of builders who contribute to its ongoing improvement and create a wealth of free libraries and tools at your disposal.

- **Cross-platform compatibility:** Write Python code as soon as possible and run it on several running structures like Windows, macOS, Linux, and even cell platforms! This flexibility saves you time and effort when growing software programs for distinctive environments.

- **Abundant libraries:** Python boasts a massive collection of external libraries, and pre-written code modules that provide functionalities for specific tasks. This huge library ecosystem saves you time from scratch and offers solutions for almost any programming venture you can imagine.

- **A supportive community:** The Python community is famed for being welcoming and helpful. There are limitless online forums, communities, and tutorials where you can get assistance, share your creations, and research from other passionate programmers.

Unleashing Your Creativity: What You Can Build with Python

With Python at your fingertips, the probabilities for advent are virtually endless. Here's a glimpse into what you can construct with this high-quality language:

Web applications: Python excels at internet development, thanks to effective frameworks like Django and Flask. You can create dynamic websites, interactive Internet services, and complicated web functions that run on the Internet.

Data Science: Python reigns supreme in the realm of data science. Libraries like NumPy, Pandas, and Matplotlib empower you to analyze and manipulate data, extract insights, and create wonderful record visualizations.

Machine Learning: Dive into the world of artificial intelligence with Python! Utilize libraries like

TensorFlow, PyTorch, and sci-kit-learn to construct smart machines that can study from data, make predictions, and automate tasks.

Automation Scripts: Python is a grasp of automation. Automate repetitive tasks on your computer, streamline workflows, and keep yourself valuable time by writing Python scripts.

Game Development: Bring your game thoughts to life with Python! While not the most common desire for high-end graphics, Python can be an amazing tool for creating exciting and enticing games, in particular when blended with libraries like Pygame.

Scientific Computing: Python is a powerful tool for scientific computing. Perform complex calculations, analyze scientific data, and create simulations with libraries like SciPy and SymPy.

Desktop Applications: Develop hassle-free laptop functions with Python's graphical consumer interface (GUI) toolkits like Tkinter, PyQt, and Kivy. Create intuitive interfaces for your software program and supply a seamless user experience.

This is simply a taste of what's possible with Python. As you delve deeper into this notable language, you may discover even more exciting purposes and find the actual energy of Python to flip your thoughts into reality.

So, are you prepared to be part of the Python revolution? In the following chapters, we are going to embark on a hands-on experience to research the fundamentals of Python programming, guiding you step-by-step from the fundamentals to constructing your personal extremely good creations.

Chapter 2: Setting Up Your Python Playground - Installing Essentials and Saying Hello to the World

Welcome to Chapter 2, the place where we will radically change your PC into a Python playground! In this chapter, we are going to inform you through the quintessential steps of putting in Python and its quintessential components, setting the stage for your programming adventures. We'll then write your first Python program, a traditional way of life that marks the opening of your journey.

Installing Python: Your Gateway to the World of Code

The first step to the use of Python is to install it on your computer. Here's a breakdown of the system for the most common operating systems:

Windows:

1. Head over to the reputable Python download website: https://www.python.org/down loads/.
2. Download the present-day secure version of Python that matches your machine architecture (32-bit or 64-bit). You can generally discover these records in your gadget settings.
3. During installation, make sure to test the field that provides Python to your device path. This permits you to run Python

commands from any listing in your command prompt.

4. Once the setup is complete, open your command instant (search for "cmd" in the Start menu) and type python --version. If the whole lot went well, you should see the mounted Python version displayed.

macOS:

There are two most important approaches to set up Python on macOS:

Using Homebrew (recommended): Homebrew is a famous bundle manager for macOS that simplifies software program installation. If you don't have Homebrew already, you can install it by way of following the directions on their website: https://brew.sh/. Once Homebrew is installed, open your terminal and run the following command:

Bash
brew install python
Use code with caution.

Using the official Python installer: Similar to Windows, you can download the contemporary Python installer from the respectable website:
https://www.python.org/downloads/
Follow the setup prompts and make sure you add Python to your PATH environment variable.
Linux:

The installation approach for Python on Linux distributions can range slightly depending on your particular version. Here's a regular guideline:

Open your terminal window.
Update your bundle lists the use of the gorgeous command for your distribution (e.g., sudo apt update for Ubuntu/Debian).
Install Python with the use of the bundle manager for your distribution (e.g., sudo apt deploy python3 for Ubuntu/Debian or sudo yum set up python3 for Fedora/CentOS).
Verifying the Installation:

Once you've installed Python, open your terminal or command prompt and type python --version (or python3 --version on some systems). If the installation was once successful, you ought to see the hooked-up Python version displayed on your screen.

Choosing Your Python Development Environment: Where the Magic Happens
Now that Python is installed, it's time to choose your development environment. This is where you may write, run, and debug your Python code. Here are a few famous options:

IDLE: IDLE is an easy and easy-to-use integrated improvement environment (IDE) that comes bundled with the default Python installation. It's a precise beginning point for novices due to its basic interface.

Visual Studio Code: This powerful and versatile code editor is a popular choice among developers for a variety of programming languages, including Python. It affords syntax highlighting, code completion, debugging tools, and a large variety of extensions specially designed for Python development.

PyCharm: If you're searching for an extra feature-rich IDE specially designed for Python, PyCharm is a super option. It offers advanced facets for large projects, together with code navigation, refactoring tools, and built-in version control support.

No count number which surroundings you choose, make sure it feels relaxed and allows you to focal point on writing code effectively.

Hello, World! - Your First Python Program

Let's write your first Python program! This traditional subculture marks a sizable milestone in your programming journey. Here's how to create a simple application that prints the iconic message "Hello, World!":

1. Open your chosen development environment.
2. Create a new Python file. You can identify something you like, but a frequent conference is hello_world.py.
3. Inside the file, kind the following line of code:

Python
```
print("Hello, World!")
```
Use code with caution.

This line of code uses the print function, a built-in function in Python that displays the message you provide within citation marks on the screen.

4. Save your Python file.
5. Now comes the moment of truth! Run your program and use the "Run" functionality in your improvement environment. Alternatively, you can navigate to the listing of the place you saved your file using your terminal or command prompt and then kind python hello_world.py

Chapter 3: The Building Blocks of Python - Understanding Variables, Data Types, and Operators

Congratulations! You've correctly established Python, written your first program, and entered the interesting world of coding. Now, it's time to delve deeper into the integral building blocks of Python programming: variables, records types, and operators. These factors are the integral ingredients that form the foundation of any Python program.

Variables: Containers for Your Data
Imagine a workbench filled with several pieces of equipment you

need for your project. In Python, variables act like labeled containers on your workbench, protecting particular pieces of information you can use during your program.

Here's how variables work in Python:

Declaring a Variable: You create a variable by assigning it a name. This title follows precise naming conventions:

It has to begin with a letter (uppercase or lowercase) or an underscore (_).
It can incorporate letters, numbers, and underscores, but no special characters (except underscores).
Python is case-sensitive, so age and Age are considered extraordinary variables.

Assigning a Value: Once you've declared a variable, you can assign it a cost using the undertaking operator (=). The value can be any kind of data, like numbers, text, or even collections of records that we will explore later.

Here's an instance of declaring and assigning a cost to a variable:

Python
```
name = "Alice"
age = 30
score = 95.5   # Can store decimal values
is_happy = True   # Can store True or False values
```
Use code with caution.

In this example, we have created four variables:

name shops a string value, "Alice".

age stores an integer value, 30, representing a complete number.

score shops a floating-point number, 95.5, which can hold decimal values.

is_happy stores a boolean value, True, indicating a logical nation (True or False).

Variable Scope: It's vital to understand the idea of variable scope. This determines the place where your variable is reachable inside your program. Variables can have neighborhood scope (accessible solely inside a unique block of code) or global scope (accessible during your entire program). We'll discover the scope in more detail in later chapters.

Data Types: Defining the Nature of Your Data

Just like equipment on your workbench has one-of-a-kind purposes, facts in Python come in quite several types. Each fact type specifies the type of records a variable can hold. Understanding data types is imperative for writing efficient and accurate Python programs. **Here are some quintessential information types in Python:**

Arithmetic Operators: These perform mathematical calculations like addition ( ), subtraction (-), multiplication (*), division (/), and modulo (%) which offers the remainder of a division.

Comparison Operators: These compare values and return boolean consequences (True or False). Examples consist of == (equal to), !=

(not equal to), < (less than), > (greater than), = (greater than or equal to).

Assignment Operators: We already saw the basic venture operator (=). Python affords mixed task operators like = (add and assign), -= (subtract and assign), and *= (multiply and assign) for concise code.

Logical Operators: These mix boolean expressions. Examples consist of and (both stipulations must be True), or (at least one situation needs to be

Chapter 4: Branching Out with Decisions: Control Flow with if, else, and Loops

In our programming ride so far, we've learned about the indispensable constructing blocks of Python – variables, information types, and operators. Now, it is time to take a step further and explore how to manipulate the drift of your program's execution. This chapter dives into two critical concepts: conditional statements with if and else, and loops for repetitive tasks.

Conditional Statements with if and else: Making Decisions
Imagine you are building software that assesses if anybody is

historically ample to vote. You would not want your software to show "Eligible to Vote" all the time. Here's the place if and else statements come into play. They enable your software to make decisions primarily based on positive conditions, directing the go-with-the-flow of execution accordingly.

The if Statement: The if statement examines a condition. If the circumstance evaluates to True, the code block indented within the if declaration is executed.
Here's the primary syntax:

Python
if condition:
    # Code to execute if the condition is True
Use code with caution.

The else Statement: The else declaration gives an alternative block of code to execute if the situation in the if assertion is False. Here's the syntax with else:

Python
```
if condition:
    # Code to execute if the condition
is True
else:
    # Code to execute if the condition
is False
```
Use code with caution.
content_copy
Example:

Python
```
age = 18

if age >= 18:
    print("You are eligible to vote.")
```

```
else:
    print("You are not eligible to vote
yet.")
```
Use code with caution.

content_copy

In this example, the program checks if the value stored in the variable age is greater than or equal to 18. If it is, the message "You are eligible to vote" is printed. Otherwise, the message "You are no longer eligible to vote yet" is displayed.

Nested if Statements: You can have nested if statements within different if or else block to create extra complicated decision-making logic.

elif Statement: Python provides the elif (else if) announcement as a way to chain more than one condition inside an if block. It allows you to take a look at alternative prerequisites if the initial circumstance is False.

Here's the syntax:

Python
```
if condition1:
    # Code to execute if condition1 is
True
elif condition2:
    # Code to execute if condition1 is
False and condition2 is True
# You can have multiple Elif
statements
else:
    # Code to execute if all conditions
are False
```
Use code with caution.
content_copy
Example:

Python

```
grade = 85

if grade >= 90:
    print("Excellent!")
elif grade >= 80:
    print("Very good!")
else:
    print("Keep practicing!")
```
Use code with caution.

This instance assigns a grade to a variable and then makes use of a collection of if and elif statements to print exclusive messages based totally on the grade value.

Loops: Automating Repetitive Tasks
Imagine you want to print the numbers from 1 to 10 ten times. Writing "print(1)" ten times would be tedious and error-prone. This is where loops come in. Loops allow you to execute a block of code many

times until a certain condition is met.

The for Loop: The for loop is used to iterate over a sequence of items. It takes a variable (often called a loop counter) that iterates through every item in the sequence, and the indented code block inside the loop executes for each item.
Here's the fundamental syntax:

```python
Python
for items in sequence:
    # Code to execute for each item in
the sequence
Use code with caution.
content_copy
```

Example:

```python
Python
# Print numbers from 1 to 10
for number in range(1, 11):
```

```
print(number)
```
Use code with caution.

In this example, the for loop iterates through a sequence of numbers generated with the aid of the range(1, 11) function. The loop counter number takes on the cost of every quantity in the sequence, and the indented code (print(number)) is executed for each iteration, printing the numbers from 1 to 10.

The while Loop: The whilst loop continues to execute a block of code as long as a sure circumstance remains True. It's beneficial when you do not comprehend earlier how many times the loop wants to run. Here's the primary syntax:

Python
```
while condition:
```

```
    # Code to execute as long as the
condition is
```
Use code with caution.
content_copy
Sources
info
github.com/YoanEnchev/Coding-Ch
amp-Blog

Chapter 5: Supercharge Your Code with Functions - Organizing Your Code Like a Pro

As your Python programs develop in complexity, maintaining your code geared up and maintainable becomes increasingly more important. Functions are your secret weapon for accomplishing this goal. They act like reusable construction blocks, encapsulating unique duties inside your program. Here's how features empower you to write clean, modular, and efficient Python code.

What are Functions? - Reusable Blocks of Code

Imagine you are constructing with LEGO bricks. Instead of having to recreate the identical complex structure every time, you can bring together a pre-built module and reuse it throughout your project. Functions work similarly in Python.

Defining a Function: You create a feature using the def keyword observed using the characteristic identity and parentheses. The indented block of code inside the function definition defines the precise movements the function will perform when called.

Here's the fundamental structure:

Python
```
def function_name(parameters):
    # Code to be executed when the
function is called
```

This code block can contain statements, calculations, and other function calls
Use code with caution.

Parameters: Parameters are like placeholders within the function's definition. When you name the function, you supply proper values (arguments) that are handed to these parameters. These arguments turn out to be reachable for use inside the function's code block.

Returning Values: Functions can optionally return a value for the usage of the return statement. This fee is dispatched and returned to the phase of your program where the feature was called.

Here's an instance of an easy feature that greets anyone with the aid of a name:

Python
```
def greet(name):
    " This function prints a greeting message."""
    message = "Hello, " + name + "!"
    print(message)

# Calling the function with an argument
greet("Alice")
```
Use code with caution.

In this example, the greet characteristic takes one parameter, name. When you name the characteristic with the argument "Alice", the price is assigned to the identified parameter inside the function. The feature then constructs a greeting message using string concatenation and prints it using the print function.

Benefits of Using Functions: Why Functions Rock

There are quite a few compelling reasons to embody functions in your Python code:

Readability and Maintainability: By breaking down your application into smaller, well-defined functions, you improve code readability and maintainability. Functions make your code greater prepared and easier to recognize for yourself and others.

Reusability: Functions are reusable constructing blocks. Once you have written and examined a function, you can call it from somewhere in your application or even from different Python programs. This saves you time and effort from rewriting the identical code repeatedly.

Modularity: Functions promote modular programming, the place where your code is divided into independent, self-contained modules. This makes it easier to debug, test, and alter specific parts of your program besides affecting the rest.

Improved Code Structure: Functions assist you shape your code logically, making it less complicated to reason about how your application works and pick out practicable issues.

Calling Functions: Putting Your Reusable Blocks to Work
Once you have described a function, you can call it from anywhere in

your software to execute the code it contains. Here's how characteristic calls work:

Function Call Syntax: You name a function using the usage of its identity accompanied by parentheses. Inside the parentheses, you can optionally supply arguments (values) that correspond to the function's parameters.
Here's the syntax:

Python
function_name(argument1, argument2, ...)
Use code with caution.

Matching Arguments to Parameters: The range and order of arguments you grant in the feature call must match the variety and order of

parameters described in the function's signature.
Example:

Python
```python
def calculate_area(length, width):
    " This function calculates the area
of a rectangle."""
    area = length * width
    return area


# Calling the function with arguments
rectangle_area = calculate_area(5, 3)  # length = 5, width = 3
print("The area of the rectangle is:", rectangle_area)
```
Use code with caution.

In this example, the calculate_area characteristic takes two parameters, size and width. When we call the characteristic with the arguments 5 and 3, they are assigned to the corresponding parameters within the function. The function calculates the area and returns the value, which is then saved in the variable rectangle_area and printed to the console.

By efficiently the usage of functions, you will be nicely on your way to writing expert and maintainable Python code. In the following chapters, we are going to explore more superior concepts in Python programming, and you may see how functions end up an even extra powerful tool for building complicated and environment-friendly programs.

Chapter 6: Working with Lists, Tuples, and Dictionaries - Powerful Data Structures for Pythonistas

As you delve deeper into the world of Python programming, you'll come across the want to organize and manage collections of data. This is the place where data buildings come into play. Python offers a range of built-in data buildings that permit you to store and manipulate data efficiently. In this chapter, we are going to explore three necessary information structures: lists, tuples, and dictionaries.

Lists: Ordered and Changeable Collections

Imagine you have a shopping list with several gadgets you need to buy. Lists in Python are similar – they are ordered collections of items that can hold exceptional information sorts like numbers, strings, or even other lists.

Creating Lists: You can create a list using rectangular brackets [] and enclose the elements inside them, separated with the aid of commas. Here's an example:

Python
shopping_list = ["apples", "bread", "milk", 2] # Mixing data types is allowed
Use code with caution.

Accessing Elements: Elements in a listing are accessed using their index, which starts from 0. The first

thing has an index of 0, the 2d factor has an index of 1, and so on.
Here's how to get entry to elements:

Python
```
first_item = shopping_list[0]   #
Accessing the first element (apples)
last_item = shopping_list[-1]   #
Accessing the last element using
negative indexing
```
Use code with caution.
content_copy

Modifying Lists: Unlike some information structures, lists are mutable, which means you can trade their contents after creation. You can alter elements, add new items, or put off present ones using quite several methods.
Here are some frequent listing amendment methods:

shopping_list.append("eggs") - Adds "eggs" to the give-up of the list.

shopping_list.insert(1, "cheese") - Inserts "cheese" at index 1.

shopping_list.remove("bread") - Removes the first prevalence of "bread".

shopping_list.pop() - Removes and returns the remaining element.

Slicing: You can extract an element of a listing of the usage of slicing. Slicing extracts a sublist primarily based on a start index (inclusive) and a quit index (exclusive).

Here's an example:

Python

```
dairy_items = shopping_list[2:4] #
Extracts "milk" and "eggs"
(elements at index 2 and 3)
```
Use code with caution.

Lists are versatile facts shaped for storing and managing ordered sequences of data. They are perfect for situations where you need to hold the tune of objects in a particular order and have the flexibility to regulate the list as needed.

Tuples: Ordered and Immutable Collections
Tuples are the structure of another integral record in Python, similar to lists in their ordered nature. However, tuples are immutable, meaning their contents can't be modified after creation.

Creating Tuples: Tuples are created using parentheses (), comparable to lists.

Here's an example:

```python
coordinates = (3, 5)   # A tuple containing coordinates
```
Use code with caution.

Accessing Elements: Element access in tuples works identically to lists, the use of indexing.

Immutability: Since tuples are immutable, you cannot adjust their elements or add/remove gadgets after creation. This immutability makes tuples ideal for situations where you want to ensure integrity and prevent unintentional changes.

Here's an attempt to adjust a tuple (resulting in an error):

Python
```
coordinates[0] = 10   # This will cause a TypeError because tuples are immutable
```
Use code with caution.

Common Tuple Operations: While you cannot regulate elements, tuples offer some useful built-in functions for working with them.
Here are some examples:

Len (coordinates) - Returns the number of elements in the tuple (2 in this case).
coordinates. count(3) - Counts the variety of occurrences of a thing (1 in this case).
Tuples are a powerful desire for representing fixed data units or

collections in the place you choose to guarantee statistics integrity. Their immutability prevents unintended modifications.

Dictionaries: Unordered Collections with Key-Value Pairs

Imagine a cell phone ebook where every entry has a title (key) associated with a smartphone range (value). Dictionaries in Python are characterized similarly. They are unordered collections of key-value pairs, the place every key is special and serves as an identifier for its corresponding value.

Creating Dictionaries: You create dictionaries using curly braces {} and enclose key-value pairs separated through colons. Keys can be strings, numbers, or tuples

(immutable), while values can be any data type.
Here's an example:

```Python
phonebook = {
    "Alice": "123-45
```
Use code with caution.

Part 2: Level Up Your Coding Skills (Intermediate Adventures Await!)

1. Data Structures and Algorithms: Understanding statistics constructions and algorithms is fundamental for writing environment-friendly and optimized code. Data buildings are integral building blocks that enable you to save and manipulate records in a structured manner. Dive deep into matters such as arrays, linked lists, stacks, queues, trees, graphs, sorting algorithms (e.g., quicksort, mergesort), searching algorithms (e.g., binary search), and dynamic programming. Learn how to analyze the time and area complexity of

algorithms to make knowledgeable decisions about which algorithm to use in different scenarios. By getting to know data structures and algorithms, you'll be able to write code that is not only correct but also performs properly in terms of velocity and memory usage.

2. Object-Oriented Programming (OOP): Object-oriented programming (OOP) is a paradigm that allows you to organize your code into reusable and maintainable components. Dive into ideas such as classes, objects, inheritance, polymorphism, and encapsulation. Practice designing and implementing OOP concepts in your code to create modular and scalable solutions. By leveraging OOP principles, you can obtain code reusability, flexibility, and less

complicated maintenance. Understanding OOP will help you shape your codebase correctly and construct software program systems that are less difficult to extend and preserve over time.

Chapter 7: Mastering Input and Output - Getting User Input and Displaying Results with Finesse

The artwork of programming involves no longer solely manipulating records within your application but also interacting with the user. In this chapter, we'll delve into the world of enter and output (I/O) in Python. You'll analyze how to correctly get consumers to enter and display program effects in a clear and user-friendly manner.

Input: Bringing the User into the Loop
Imagine you are constructing software that calculates the vicinity

of a rectangle. To make it interactive, you'll desire the consumer to grant the size and width values. This is the place where consumer input comes into play.

The input() Function: Python affords the built-in input() feature to get user input from the console. When called, the input() characteristic pauses your program's execution and displays a prompt (optional message) on the screen. The person then kinds their enter and presses Enter. The input() feature captures what the user typed and returns it as a string.
Here's an example:

```python
Python
name = input("What is your name? ")
print("Hello,", name)
```

Use code with caution.

In this example, the input() feature prompts the consumer with the message "What is your name? ". The consumer sorts their name and presses Enter. The input() feature captures the user's enter (as a string) and assigns it to the variable name. The application then proceeds to greet the consumer by way of name.

Important Note: By default, the input() function continually returns a string, even if the user enters a number. You might also want to convert the enter to an extraordinary records kind (like integer or float) if your software requires numerical calculations.

Type Conversion: Transforming User Input

As cited earlier, the input() feature returns a string. If you need to function calculations or comparisons with the user's input, you'll regularly want to convert it to the suitable information type. Here are some common type conversion functions:

int(string) - Converts a string to an integer (whole number).
float(string) - Converts a string to a floating-point quantity (decimal number).

Here's an example with type conversion:

```
length_str = input("Enter the length of the rectangle: ")
width_str = input("Enter the width of the rectangle: ")
```

```
# Convert strings to integers for
calculations
length = int(length_str)
width = int(width_str)

area = length * width
print("The area of the rectangle
is:", area)
```
Use code with caution.

In this example, the program prompts the user for the length and width of a rectangle. The input() feature captures the user's enter as strings. We then use the int() characteristic to convert these strings to integers before performing the vicinity calculation.

Output: Displaying Results with Clarity

The other half of the I/O equation is output. This is how your application communicates the results of its calculations or movements again to the user. Python provides quite a few methods to display output on the console.

The print() Function: The print() characteristic is the most imperative way to display output in Python. You can pass any statistics type (strings, numbers, variables) to the print() function, and it will be displayed on the console.
Here's an example:

```
Python
message = "Hello, world!"
print(message)
Use code with caution.
```

Formatting Output: The print() function approves for simple formatting and the usage of string formatting techniques. You can use f-strings (introduced in Python 3.6) or the older string formatting method with the modulo operator (%). F-strings are typically regarded as greater readable and maintainable.

Here's an instance of the use of f-strings:

```python
name = "Alice"
age = 30
print(f"Hello, {name}! You are {age} years old.")
```
Use code with caution.

This example uses of-strings to embed variables (name and age) at once within the string, resulting in an extra readable and dynamic output message.

Newline Characters (\n): By default, the print() characteristic inserts a newline personality (\n) after every printed value. You can manipulate this behavior by including the give-up argument to the print() function.
Here's an example:

Python
```
print("Hello", end=" ")
print("World!")
```
Use code with caution.

This code will print "Hello World!" on the same line due to the fact the stop argument in the first print() characteristic is set to a house (").

By gaining knowledge of consumer input and output techniques, you'll be in a position to create interactive Python programs that interact with customers and provide clear feedback.

Chapter 8: Loops Like a Boss - for and while Loops for Efficient Repetition

In our programming ride so far, we have encountered the thought of loops – effective tools for automating repetitive tasks. This chapter delves deeper into the two quintessential loop kinds in Python: for loops and whilst loops. You'll study how to leverage them effectively to write concise and efficient code.

The Versatile for Loop: Iterating Over Sequences
Imagine you have a listing of names and you desire to greet every man or woman individually. Writing a

separate print declaration for every title would be tedious and error-prone. This is where loops shine.

Basic Structure: The for loop iterates over a sequence of objects (like a list, string, or tuple). It takes a variable (often known as a loop counter) that takes on the fee of each item in the sequence in the course of each iteration. The indented code block within the loop executes for every item.
Here's the fundamental syntax:

Python
for items in sequence:
    # Code to execute for each item in the sequence
Use code with caution.
content_copy
Example:

Python
names = ["Alice", "Bob", "Charlie"]

```python
for name in names:
  print(f"Hello, {name}!")
```
Use code with caution.

In this example, the for loop iterates over the names list. In each iteration, the loop counter title takes on the fee of each name in the list ("Alice", "Bob", and "Charlie"). The indented code block (print(f"Hello, {name}!")) is performed for each name, resulting in greetings for each person.

Iterating Over Strings: loops can also iterate over the characters in a string.
Here's an example:

Python
message = "Hello, world!"

```python
for char in the message:
    print(char, end=" ")
```
Use code with caution.

This code iterates over every personality in the message string, printing every personality followed using a space (using the end argument in print).

The Indefatigable whilst Loop: Looping Until a Condition is Met
Imagine you're taking part in a guessing sport, the place where the consumer wishes to guess a secret number. You would not comprehend formally how many guesses it will take. This is the place where loops come in handy.

Basic Structure: The whilst loop continues to execute a block of code as lengthy as a positive circumstance stays True. The loop examines the condition before every iteration. If the condition is False, the loop terminates.

Here's the basic syntax:

Python
```
while condition:
    # Code to execute as long as the condition is True
```
Use code with caution.
content_copy
Example:

Python
```
secret_number = 7
guess_count = 0

while guess_count < 3:
```

```
    guess = int(input("Guess the
secret number (between 1 and 10):
"))
    guess_count += 1  # Increment
guess count after each attempt

  if guess == secret_number:
        print("Congratulations! You
guessed the number!")
        break  # Exit the loop if the
guess is correct
    else:
      print("Try again!")

if guess_count == 3:  # Check if all
attempts are used
      print("Sorry, you ran out of
guesses. The secret number was",
secret_number)
```

Use code with caution.

This code implements a guessing sport with at most three attempts.

The while loop continues as long as guess_count is less than 3 Inside the loop, the consumer is brought about for a guess, and the bet relied on is incremented. If the guess is correct, the loop exits the usage of break. Otherwise, an error message is displayed. After the loop exits, a final message is proven based on whether the person guessed the variety or not.

Choosing the Right Loop: for vs. while

While each for and whilst loops are effective tools, appreciation of the key differences helps you pick the terrific one for your task:

Use for loops: When you know previously how many times you want to iterate or when you're working with a sequence of items.

Use while loops: When you don't comprehend the genuine quantity of iterations beforehand, the loop continues as long as a circumstance remains True.

Example:

Printing numbers from 1 to 5: Use a for loop due to the fact you know the genuine range of iterations (5).

Python
import random

secret
Use code with caution.

Chapter 9: Debugging: Your Secret Weapon for Flawless Python Code

As you embark on your Python programming journey, you may inevitably encounter errors and unexpected behavior in your code. These glitches, often referred to as bugs, can be frustrating but are an herbal phase of the studying process. The top news is that Python provides a sturdy set of debugging equipment and methods to help you identify, understand, and fix these bugs. This chapter equips you with the understanding and techniques to emerge as a debugging ninja!

Understanding Errors: Different Types of Glitches

There are two primary categories of mistakes you may encounter in Python:

- **Syntax Errors:** These are violations of Python's grammar rules. They happen when you mistype keywords, overlook colons or parentheses, or make different structural mistakes. Syntax errors forestall your software from even running and are commonly handy to perceive and fix.

Here's an example:

```
Python
print("Hello world!    # Missing closing parenthesis
Use code with caution.
```

This code will end in a syntax error because the print declaration is missing a closing parenthesis.

- **Runtime Errors:** These blunders manifest whilst your application is genuinely running. They can arise due to a variety of reasons, such as trying to get admission to a non-existent element in a list, performing calculations with incompatible fact types, or encountering sudden inputs. Runtime errors can be trickier to pinpoint due to the fact they may additionally not appear until the software reaches a positive point of execution.

Here's an example:

Python

```
numbers = [1, 2, 3]
print(numbers[4])    # Trying to
access an index out of range
```
Use code with caution.

This code will result in a runtime error (IndexError) due to the fact you're attempting to get admission to the element at index 4, which doesn't exist in the list numbers (it solely has three elements).

Essential Debugging Tools: Pinpointing the Problem
Python presents several built-in equipment that are useful resources in the debugging process:

The print() Function: Your trusty friend, the print() function, is worthwhile for debugging. You can strategically locate print statements in the course of your code to check

out the values of variables at exclusive points in your program's execution. This helps you music how facts change and perceive the place things may be going wrong.
Here's an example:

Python
```
x = 5
y = 10

# Print the values before the calculation
print("x before calculation:", x)
print("y before calculation:", y)

z = x / y  # Potential division by zero error

# Print the value after the calculation (if the division happens)
print("z after calculation:", z)
```
Use code with caution.

The input() Function: Similar to print(), the input() feature can be used in the course of debugging to pause your program and ask the consumer for unique input. This can be useful for checking out distinct eventualities or setting apart the issue.

Debuggers: Python presents several debuggers, like the built-in pdb module or graphical debuggers like PyCharm's debugger. This equipment enables you to step through your code line by line, investigate variable values at every step, and set breakpoints (stopping points) to pause execution at particular points.

Debugging Strategies: A Systematic Approach

Here are some high-quality debugging techniques to handle mistakes efficiently:

Read the Error Message Carefully: The error message displayed with the aid of Python regularly affords precious clues about the area and nature of the error. Pay shut interest to the error type, the line range, the place it occurs, and any additional small print provided.

Simplify Your Code: If you're dealing with a complicated program, try to isolate the tricky area by breaking it down into smaller, testable chunks. This makes it easier to pinpoint the error source.

Use Comments: Adding remarks to your code can explain your idea procedure and the functionality of one-of-a-kind sections. This can be helpful when revisiting your code later or when anyone wants to apprehend it.

Test Incrementally: As you write your code, test it often after adding new functionality. This helps capture mistakes early on and prevents them from accumulating.
Leverage Online Resources: The Python neighborhood is sizable and helpful. Don't hesitate to search online forums or documentation for solutions to frequent errors. You might find any person else has already encountered the same issue and located a fix.

Beyond Debugging: Preventive Measures
While debugging is a critical skill, there are ways to write code that is

less susceptible to errors in the first place:

Use Clear and Meaningful Variable Names: Descriptive variable names make your code less complicated to study and understand, which can help you perceive practicable problems early on.

Proper Indentation: Python relies on indentation to outline code blocks. Inconsistent indentation can lead to logical errors that would possibly be tough to spot at first glance.

Chapter 10: Working with Files - Storing and Retrieving Data Like a Champion

As your Python programs evolve, you'll probably need to manipulate data that persists beyond the program's execution. This is the place documents come in. Files act as exterior storage containers for your data, allowing you to retail data and retrieve it later, even if you terminate your program. In this chapter, you may delve into the world of file dealing in Python, getting to know how to examine from, write to, and manipulate several file types.

Understanding File I/O: Input and Output with Files

File copying includes two vital operations: reading records from a file and writing information to a file. These operations are analogous to how you engage with exterior gadgets like your keyboard (input) and reveal (output).

File Modes: When working with files, you need to specify a mode in which you open the file. The two most frequent modes are:

'r' (read mode): Opens the file for analyzing existing content. Attempting to write to a file opened in examine mode will end in an error.

'w' (write mode): Opens the file for writing. Any existing content material in the file will be overwritten.

Here's an example of opening a file for reading:

Python
```
with open("data.txt", "r") as file:
    # Read content from the file
    file_content = file.read()
    print(file_content)
```
Use code with caution.

In this example, we open the file "output.txt" in write mode ("w"). Any current content in the file will be erased. We then use the file.write() approach to write the string data_to_write to the file.

Common File Operations: Essential Techniques
Python gives more than a few methods for interacting with files:

file.read(): Reads the entire content material of the file into a string.

file.readline(): Reads a single line from the file and returns it as a string (including the newline character).

file. deadlines (): Reads all strains from the file and returns them as a list of strings, the place every aspect in the list represents a line.

file.write(data): Writes the specified records (string) to the file.

Example:

Python
```
with open("data.txt", "r") as file:
    # Read line by line
    for line in the file.deadlines():
        print(line. strip())  # Remove
trailing newline character
Use code with caution.
```

This code reads the file "data.txt" line by line for the usage of a for loop. The file. readlines() technique returns a list of lines, and we iterate via each line using the for loop. The strip() approach is used to cast off the trailing newline personality from each line before printing.

Important Considerations: File Paths and Error Handling
When working with files, keep these factors in mind:

File Paths: You need to specify the correct course (location) of the file you favor to open. This route can be relative (based on the location of your Python script) or absolute (specifying the entire listing structure).
Here's an example of a relative path:

Python
```
with open("data.txt", "r") as file:  #
Assuming "data.txt" is in the same
directory
    # Read the file
```
Use code with caution.

Error Handling: File operations can probably come across errors, such as attempting to open a non-existent file or writing to a read-only file. It's a suitable exercise to include error error-handlinghanisms, and the usage of try-except blocks to gracefully deal with these situations and forestall your program from crashing.

Here's an example of error handling:

Python
```python
try:
    with open("data.txt", "r") as file:
        # Read the file
        file_content = file.read()
except FileNotFoundError:
        print("Error: File 'data.txt' not
found.")
```
Use code with caution.

Chapter 11: Embrace the Power of Objects and Classes - Building Reusable Code with Style

In our programming trip so far, we've explored critical constructing blocks like variables, fact types, functions, and control flow. As your applications end up greater complex, you'll encounter the want to manipulate data and performance in a more geared-up and reusable way. This is where object-oriented programming (OOP) comes into play. This chapter introduces you to the world of objects and training in Python, empowering you to write cleaner, extra-maintainable, and modular code.

Object-Oriented Programming (OOP): A Paradigm Shift

OOP is a programming paradigm that revolves around objects. An object encapsulates facts (attributes) and the related moves (methods) that can function on that data. Imagine a vehicle – it has attributes like color, model, and speed. It additionally has techniques like acceleration, braking, and, unturning. In OOP, an auto would be an object, and its attributes and techniques would be described within a blueprint referred to as a class.

Classes: Blueprints for Creating Objects

A class acts as a template or blueprint that defines the homes (attributes) and behaviors (methods) of its objects. Here's the fundamental structure of a class:

Python
```python
class ClassName:
    # Attributes (data)
    attribute1 = value1
    attribute2 = value2

    # Methods (functions)
    def method1(self):
        # Code to be executed

    def method2(self, argument):
        # Code to be executed with an
argument
```
Use code with caution.

Explanation:

ClassName: This is the name you provide to your class. It ought to be descriptive and comply with Python naming conventions (PascalCase).

Attributes: These are variables that outline the characteristics of an object created from the class. They can be initialized inside the type definition or assigned values later.

Methods: These are functions described within the classification that outline the object's behavior. They can get the right of entry to and manipulate the object's attributes. The first argument in an approach definition is commonly self, which refers to the cutting-edge object instance.
Example:

Python
class Car:

```python
    color = "black"  # Class attribute
(shared by all instances)

    def __init__(self, model, year):
# Special method called constructor
        self.model = model  # Instance
attribute (unique to each object)
        self. year = year

    define accelerate(self):
        print(f"The {self. model} car is
accelerating!")

# Create objects (instances) of the
Car class
car1 = Car("Tesla Model S", 2024)
car2 = Car("Honda Civic", 2020)

car1.accelerate()   # Output: The
Tesla Model S car is accelerating!
print(car2.model)  # Output: Honda
Civic
```
Use code with caution.

Object-Oriented Concepts: Diving Deeper

As you delve deeper into OOP, you will come upon more advanced concepts:

Inheritance: Inheritance allows you to create new classes (subclasses) that inherit attributes and techniques from existing instructions (parent classes). This promotes code reuse and permits specialization.

Polymorphism: Polymorphism approves objects of special training to respond to the equal technique name in special ways. This improves code flexibility and reusability.

These concepts are constructed upon the foundation of objects and classes, allowing you to create even extra effective and versatile Python programs.

Chapter 12: Python for the Real World: Exploring Popular Libraries for Beginners (Games, Data Science, and More!)

Python's authentic magic lies in its full-size ecosystem of libraries. These pre-written collections of code supply effective tools and functionalities for several tasks, permitting you to focus on the trouble at hand rather than reinventing the wheel. This chapter explores some of the most famous Python libraries for beginners, labeled utilizing their common use cases.

Game Development: Bringing Your Ideas to Life

Pygame: A beginner-friendly library for developing 2D games. Pygame provides a simple API for coping with graphics, sound effects, input, and animation. It's an awesome starting point for every person who needs to learn the fundamentals of sports development in Python.
Here's a simple instance of growing a moving circle in Pygame:

Python
```
import pygame

# Initialize Pygame
pygame. init()

# Set screen dimensions
screen_width = 800
screen_height = 600
```

```python
screen        =        pygame.
display.set_mode((screen_width,
screen_height))

# Set window title
pygame.   display.set_caption("My
First Pygame Game")

# Circle properties
circle_x = screen_width // 2
circle_y = screen_height // 2
circle_radius = 50
circle_color = (255, 0, 0)   # Red
color

# Game loop
running = True
while running:
    # Check for events (like closing
the window)
        for the event in pygame.
event.get():
    if event.type == pygame.QUIT:
```

```python
            running = False

        # Clear the screen before drawing
    a new content
        screen.fill((255, 255, 255))   #
    White background

        # Draw the circle
            pygame.  draw.circle(screen,
    circle_color,  (circle_x,  circle_y),
    circle_radius)

        # Update the display
        pygame. display.flip()

    # Quit Pygame
    pygame. quit()
```

Use code with caution.

PyOpenGL: For those who desire to challenge 3D game development, PyOpenGL provides a Python interface for the OpenGL photos library. It permits you to create 3D models, textures, lighting fixture effects, and complicated interactions, opening doors to extra immersive game experiences.

Data Science: Unveiling Insights from Data

NumPy: The foundation of many statistics science libraries in Python. NumPy gives effective tools for numerical computations, multi-dimensional arrays (matrices), linear algebra operations, and random wide variety generation. It's necessary for working with massive datasets efficiently.

Here's an instance of creating a NumPy array and performing basic operations:

Python
import numpy as np

```python
# Create a NumPy array
data = np. array([1, 2, 3, 4, 5])

# Print the array
print(data)  # Output: [1 2 3 4 5]

# Get the shape (dimensions) of the array
print(data. shape)   # Output: (5,)
(one-dimensional array with 5
elements)

# Calculate the sum of elements
total_sum = np. sum(data)
print(total_sum)  # Output: 15
```
Use code with caution.
content_copy

Pandas: Often referred to as the "workhorse" of facts science, Pandas excels at information manipulation and analysis. It presents powerful statistics constructions like Series (one-dimensional labeled arrays) and data frames (two-dimensional labeled facts with rows and columns). Pandas allow efficient information cleaning, filtering, grouping, and aggregation.

Here's an example of growing a Pandas Series and performing simple operations:

```python
Python
import pandas as PD

# Create a Series from a list
data = pd.Series([100, 200, 300, 400], index=["Apple", "Banana", "Orange", "Grape"])

# Print the Series
print(data) # Output:
# Apple    100
```

```
# Banana   200
# Orange   300
# Grape    400
#: int64

# Access data by index
apple_price = data["Apple"]
print(apple_price)  # Output: 100

# Get descriptive statistics
print(data. describe())   # Shows
summary statistics like mean,
median, etc.
```
Use code with caution.

Matplotlib and Seaborn: Visualization plays a necessary position in statistics science. Matplotlib is an integral library for creating static, publication-quality plots of several kinds (line charts, bar charts, histograms, etc.).

Part 3: Python Projects to Showcase Your Skills (Become a Coding Rockstar!)

One of the pleasant methods to reveal your coding abilities and stand out as a developer is via working on real-world projects. Building tasks not only helps you follow the ideas you've discovered but also showcases your problem-solving abilities, creativity, and coding proficiency. In this section, we'll discover some interesting Python venture thoughts that you can work on to exhibit your capabilities and end up a coding rockstar!

1. Web Scraper:

- Build a net scraper with the use of Python's libraries like BeautifulSoup and requests to extract records from websites.
- Create a script that scrapes information such as news articles, product prices, or weather forecasts from precise websites.
- Learn about net scraping ethics and first-class practices to ensure your scraper behaves responsibly.

2. Data Visualization Tool:
- Use libraries like Matplotlib or Seaborn to create interactive visualizations of record sets.
- Develop a tool that allows users to upload their data and generate insightful graphs, charts, and plots.
- Explore exclusive sorts of visualizations, such as bar graphs, pie charts, scatter plots, and

heatmaps, to current statistics effectively.

3. Chatbot:
- Implement a chatbot using libraries like NLTK or spaCy for herbal language processing.
- Design a conversational interface that can answer user queries, grant recommendations, or engage in casual conversations.
- Experiment with computing device learning strategies to decorate the chatbot's understanding and responses over time.

4. Task Automation Script:
- Create a script that automates repetitive duties such as file management, records processing, or device maintenance.

- Use Python's built-in modules like os, shuttle, or subprocess to engage with the working device and execute commands.
- Schedule your automation script to run at unique intervals with the use of equipment like cron or Windows Task Scheduler.

5. Machine Learning Model:
- Develop a desktop studying mannequin with the use of famous libraries like scikit-learn or TensorFlow.
- Choose a dataset (e.g., Iris dataset, MNIST handwritten digits) and build a predictive mannequin for classification or regression tasks.
- Experiment with exceptional algorithms (e.g., choice trees, help vector machines, neural networks) and hyperparameter tuning to enhance mannequin performance.

6. Game Development:
- Create an easy sport using Pygame or other recreation development libraries in Python.
- Build basic video games like Snake, Tic-Tac-Toe, or Pong to exhibit your game development skills.
- Implement facets such as scoring systems, person input handling, collision detection, and recreation states to make your game enticing and interactive.

7. API Integration Project:
- Integrate with third-party APIs (e.g., Twitter API, Google Maps API, Spotify API) to get admission to exterior information and services.
- Develop a utility that interacts with APIs to operate duties like fetching climate information,

posting tweets, or retrieving music recommendations.

- Handle authentication, error handling, fee limiting, and data parsing while working with APIs.

8. Personal Portfolio Website:
- Create a personal portfolio website using Flask or Django to showcase your projects, skills, and resume.
- Design a fascinating and responsive website with sections for challenge descriptions, tech stack used, and hyperlinks to GitHub repositories.
- Include elements like contact forms, social media integration, and weblog sections to interact with traffic and spotlight your expertise.

By working on these Python projects, you'll now not only sharpen your coding abilities but also construct a sturdy portfolio that demonstrates your skills to plausible employers or collaborators. Remember to record your tasks well, write clean and readable code, and actively search for remarks from peers to consistently enhance your craft. With dedication and persistence, you'll soon emerge as a coding rockstar in the Python programming world!

Chapter 13: Build Your First Game: From Simple to Addictive with Python

Welcome to the exciting world of game improvement with Python! In this chapter, we will embark on a trip to create a simple yet engaging game, step-by-step. By following along, you may obtain a practical ride with core sport development ideas and the energy of the Pygame library.

The Game: It's All About the Falling Square

For our first project, we will build a game called "Falling Square." The objective is to manage a rectangular use of the arrow keys and forestall it from falling off the bottom of the screen. Sounds simple, right? But as you progress, the recreation will gradually introduce challenges to keep you hooked. Here's a breakdown of the functionalities we will implement:

Game Window: We'll create a visual interface using Pygame to show the game factors (square, background).
Player Control: The player will be able to go the square left and proper using the left and right arrow keys.
Game Loop: We'll establish a non-stop loop that updates the sports nation (square's position), exams for collisions, and redraws the screen.
Increasing Difficulty: As time progresses, the speed at which the rectangular falls will progressively

increase, making it more challenging to control.

Game Over: If the square falls off the bottom of the screen, the recreation will end, and the player will see a "Game Over" message.

Setting Up the Stage: Installation and Imports

Before diving into the code, make sure you have Python and Pygame set up on your system. You can generally install them using your system's bundle supervisor or with the aid of downloading them from the official websites.

Once you're set-up, let's create a Python file for our game. Here, we'll import the quintessential libraries and outline some preliminary constants:

Python
import pygame

```python
# Define some colors
BLACK = (0, 0, 0)
WHITE = (255, 255, 255)

# Set screen dimensions
screen_width = 800
screen_height = 600
```
Use code with caution.

We import the pygame library and define constants for colors (black and white) and display dimensions. These constants will be used throughout our recreation code to hold consistency.

Bringing the Game to Life: Core Mechanics

Now comes the exciting phase – constructing the game's core functionalities!

1. Initialize Pygame:

```
Python
pygame. init()

# Create the game screen
screen              =              pygame.
display.set_mode((screen_width,
screen_height))

# Set the window title
pygame.
display.set_caption("Falling
Square")
```
Use code with caution.

Here, we initialize Pygame, create the game window using pygame.display.set_mode, and set a caption for the window using pygame.display.set_caption.

2. Define the Player (Square):

Python
```
# Player square properties
square_size = 50
square_x = screen_width // 2   # Start in the center horizontally
square_y = screen_height // 2   # Start in the center vertically
square_color = WHITE
```
Use code with caution.

We define variables for the participant square's size, initial position (center of the screen), and color.

3. Game Loop:

The recreation loop is the coronary heart of our game. It continually updates the sports state, checks for consumer input, and redraws the screen. Here's a primary structure:

```python
Python
# Game loop variable
running = True

# Clock object for controlling frame rate
clock = pygame. time.Clock()
game_speed = 5  # Initial speed of the falling square

while running:
    # Check for events (like closing the window)
    for the event in pygame. event.get():
        if event.type == pygame.QUIT:
            running = False
```

```python
    # Handle player input (arrow
keys)
    keys = pygame.key.get_pressed()
        if keys[pygame.K_LEFT] and
square_x > 0:  # Move left if within
bounds
        square_x -= 5
        if keys[pygame.K_RIGHT] and
square_x  <  screen_width  -
square_size:  # Move right if within
bounds
        square_x += 5

    # Update square position based on
game speed
    square_y += game_speed

        # Check for collision with the
bottom of the screen (game over)
        if square_y + square_size >
screen_height:
```

```
        running = False  # End the game
loop

        # Clear the screen before drawing
a new content
        screen.fill(BLACK
Use code with caution.
```

Chapter 14: Conquer Text Analysis: Extracting Meaning from Words (Sentiment Analysis for Fun!)

Have you ever wondered what the general sentiment is in the back of a large collection of online reviews, tweets, or social media posts? Sentiment analysis, a subfield of natural language processing (NLP), tackles this very challenge. Its objective is to recognize the emotional tone of a piece of textual content – whether it is positive, negative, or neutral. In this chapter, we are going to delve into the world of sentiment analysis using Python libraries and discover how to find hidden feelings inside textual content data.

Understanding Sentiment Analysis: Unveiling the Emotional Landscape Sentiment analysis can be utilized in more than a few scenarios:

Customer Reviews: Businesses can analyze customer opinions to recognize purchaser satisfaction, perceive areas for improvement, and achieve insights into product perception.

Social Media Monitoring: Brands can monitor social media mentions to gauge public sentiment in the direction of their products, campaigns, or manufacturer image.

Market Research: By analyzing online discussions and forums, researchers can recognize consumer opinions and preferences associated with particular merchandise or topics.

There are two most important techniques for sentiment analysis:

- Lexicon-Based Approach: This technique relies on pre-built sentiment lexicons – massive dictionaries that map phrases to their sentiment rankings (positive, negative, or neutral). The sentiment rating of a text is calculated by considering the sentiment scores of the person's words it contains.

- Machine Learning Approach: This method makes use of machine studying algorithms trained on large datasets of labeled textual content data. These algorithms analyze patterns in text that correlate with sentiment and can acquire greater accuracy than lexicon-based methods.

While computer learning procedures can be very powerful, they frequently require greater complicated setup and facts preparation. In this chapter, we'll center our attention on a less complicated lexicon-based strategy: the use of the TextBlob library in Python.

TextBlob: Your Friendly Text Analysis Toolkit

TextBlob is an effortless Python library for processing textual data. It provides a range of functionalities for tasks like sentiment analysis, classification, tokenization (splitting textual content into words), and more. Here's how to install TextBlob:

Bash
pip install text blob
Use code with caution.

Once installed, you can import TextBlob in your Python code:

Python
from text blob import TextBlob
Use code with caution.

Building a Basic Sentiment Analyzer: Let's Get Coding!

Now comes the exciting part – constructing an easy sentiment analyzer with the use of TextBlob. Here's a step-by-step breakdown:

Define Sentiment Lexicon:
We can create a simple sentiment lexicon as a dictionary, where keys are words and values are their sentiment ratings (positive = 1, terrible = -1, impartial = 0).

Python
```
sentiment_lexicon = {
    "great": 1,
    "super": 1,
    "fantastic": 1,
    "bad": -1,
    "terrible": -1,
    "horrible": -1,
}
```

Use code with caution.

Analyze Text Sentiment:
Here's a feature that takes a piece of text as input and returns its standard sentiment score based totally on our lexicon:

Python
```python
def calculate_sentiment(text):
    """
    Analyzes the sentiment of a text
    using a sentiment lexicon.

    Args:
        text: The text to analyze (string).

    Returns:
        A float value representing the
        sentiment score (positive: > 0,
        negative: < 0, neutral: 0).
    """
```

```
text = TextBlob(text)  # Create a
TextBlob object from the text
sentiment_score = 0
words = text.words  # Split the text
into words

for word in words:
            if word. lower() in
sentiment_lexicon:  # Check if word
is in the lexicon (case-insensitive)
                sentiment_score +=
sentiment_lexicon[word. lower()]

return sentiment_score
```
Use code with caution.

This function first creates a TextBlob object from the input text. It then iterates through the words in the textual content and assesses if each word (converted to lowercase) exists in our sentiment lexicon. If a phrase is located in the lexicon, its corresponding sentiment score is introduced to the typical sentiment score. Finally, the characteristic returns the complete sentiment rating for the text.

Testing Our Analyzer:
Let's strive out our sentiment analyzer with some sample sentences:

```python
Python
text1 = "This movie was fantastic!"
text2 = "The service at this restaurant was terrible."
text3 = "This product is just okay, nothing special."

sentiment1                          =
calculate_sentiment(text1)
sentiment2                          =
calculate_sentiment(text2)
```

```python
sentiment3                    =
calculate_sentiment(text3)

print("Sentiment score for", text1,
":", sentiment1)  # Output:
```
Use code with caution.

Chapter 15: Become a Data Visualization Whiz: Creating Charts and Graphs with Python

Data visualization is a vital talent for records scientists and absolutely everyone who wishes to speak data effectively. It involves developing visual representations of data, such as charts and graphs, to assist humans in apprehending patterns, trends, and relationships within the data. In this chapter, we are going to explore the power of Python libraries like Matplotlib and Seaborn to create informative and visually attractive facts visualizations.

The Power of Visualization: Why Charts and Graphs Matter

Data visualization presents several advantages over uncooked data tables:

Improved Comprehension: Visual representations make it less difficult for human talent to grasp complex patterns and relationships inside data.

Enhanced Communication: Charts and graphs can efficaciously speak insights and tendencies to a wider audience, even those bearing a robust statistical background.

Identification of Anomalies: Visualizations can assist perceive outliers, inconsistencies, and surprising patterns in the information that would possibly go ignored in tables.

Data Storytelling: Compelling visualizations can inform a story with the data, making it extra attractive and memorable for viewers.

Matplotlib: The Foundational Library for Data Visualization in Python

Matplotlib is a critical library in Python for creating several static, publication-quality visualizations. It presents a huge variety of plot types, including:

Line charts: Ideal for showing traits or modifications over time.

Bar charts: Useful for comparing classes or quantities.

Scatter plots: Effective for visualizing relationships between two variables.

Histograms: Depict the distribution of information factors inside a particular range.

Here's a primary example of growing a line chart with Matplotlib:

Python
import matplotlib. as plt

```
# Sample data (lists)
x = [1, 2, 3, 4, 5]
y = [2, 4, 5, 4, 6]

# Create the line chart
plt. plot(x, y)

# Add labels and title
plt.label("X-axis")
plt. label("Y-axis")
plt. title("Line Chart Example")

# Show the plot
```

```
plt. show()
```
Use code with caution.

This code creates a line chart for the usage of the plot. plot function, specifying the x and y facts as lists. It then provides labels for the axes and a title for the chart of the usage of the plot. , plt. , and plt. title, respectively. Finally, plt. show shows the generated plot.

Seaborn: Building on Matplotlib for Enhanced Visualization

Seaborn is a high-level library built on top of Matplotlib that gives a more concise and aesthetically eye-catching way to create statistical graphics. It offers themes, shade palettes, and pre-built functions for several chart types, making it less complicated to

produce   publication-ready
visualizations.

Here's an example of creating a
scatter plot with Seaborn:

Python
import seaborn as sns

```python
# Sample data (as a pandas
DataFrame)
data = sns.load_dataset("iris")   #
Load a built-in dataset
x = data["sepal_length"]
y = data["sepal_width"]

# Create the scatter plot with
color-coded species
sns. scatterplot(x, y, hue="species",
data=data, palette="deep")

# Add a title
```

```python
plt.title("Scatter Plot of Iris Sepal Length vs. Width")

# Show the plot
plt. show()
```
Use code with caution.

This code first imports Seaborn (sns). It then hundreds of the built-in "iris" datasets for the usage of SNS.load_dataset and extracts the sepal size and width records into separate variables (x and y). The SNS. A scatterplot feature is used to create the scatter plot, specifying the x and y data, color-coding by species (hue), and the use of the "deep" color palette. Finally, a title is brought using plt. title and the plot is displayed with the plot. show.

Seaborn gives a rich set of features in past scatter plots, including:

Bar charts with error bars to characterize uncertainty in the data. Violin plots show the distribution of records along their median and quartiles. Heatmaps to visualize relationships between more than one variable as a color-coded matrix. By leveraging Matplotlib and Seaborn, you can create a large variety of informative and visually attractive information visualizations in Python, empowering you to correctly speak insights from your information analysis.

Beyond the Basics: Exploring Advanced Techniques

As you develop in information visualization, you can discover superior methods to beautify your visualizations:

Customization: Both Matplotlib and Seaborn offer massive customization alternatives for fine-tuning the appearance of your charts, such as changing colors, line styles, marker shapes, and axis formatting.
Interactive Visualization Libraries:

Chapter 16: Automate Tedious Tasks: Write Python Scripts to Save You Time

Do you spend an extensive amount of time on repetitive duties on your computer? Manually renaming files, copying and pasting statistics between spreadsheets, or internet scraping statistics from identical internet sites each day can be soul-crushing and time-consuming. The suitable information is that Python can be your hero! In this chapter, we'll explore how to automate these tedious duties using Python scripts, liberating your treasured time for more creative and strategic endeavors.

The Power of Automation: Why Scripts Are Your New Best Friend

Automating repetitive tasks with Python scripts affords various benefits:

Increased Efficiency: Scripts can execute tasks an awful lot faster than you can manually, allowing you to complete more work in much less time.

Reduced Errors: Manual tasks are susceptible to human error. Scripts, once written and tested, can be executed constantly and accurately.

Improved Consistency: Scripts make sure duties are carried out in the same way each time, leading to steady results.

Freed Up Time: By automating repetitive tasks, you free up your time to center your attention on extra necessary activities that require human creativity and judgment.

Building Your First Automation Script: A Step-by-Step Guide
Let's walk through the system of growing a Python script to automate a simple assignment – renaming a batch of files in a specific directory.

1. Define the Task:

Imagine you have a folder stuffed with picture archives named "IMG_0001.jpg," "IMG_0002.jpg," and so on. You choose to rename them sequentially with a descriptive prefix, like "vacation_photo_1.jpg," "vacation_photo_2.jpg," etc.

2. Import Necessary Libraries:

We'll use the os library to interact with the running system's file system.

Python
import os
Use code with caution.

3. Define the Script Logic:

Here's the core functionality of the script:

Python
# Set the directory containing the files
directory = "/path/to/your/images"
# Replace with your actual directory path

Starting number for the new filenames

```
start_number = 1

# Loop through all files in the
directory
for filename in os. listdir(directory):
  # Check if it's an image file (adjust
the extension if needed)
  if filename.ends with(".jpg"):
    # Create the new filename with
descriptive prefix and sequential
number
            new_filename    =
f"vacation_photo_{start_number}
.jpg"
    start_number += 1  # Increment
the counter for the next file

    # Construct the full paths for old
and new filenames
            old_path    =    os.
path.join(directory, filename)
            new_path    =    os.
path.join(directory, new_filename)
```

```
# Rename the file
os. rename(old_path, new_path)

print("Files              renamed
successfully!")
Use code with caution.
```

Explanation:

We outline the directory direction containing the files.
We set a beginning range for the new filenames.
The script iterates through all documents in the listing with the use of OS
It examines if the filename ends with ".jpg" (modify the extension if wished for your file type).
The script constructs a new filename with the preferred prefix

and increments the counter for subsequent files.

It builds the full paths for each of the historic and new filenames with the usage of os.path.join.

Finally, it uses os. rename to rename the file from its ancient identity to the new name.

Once all files are processed, the script prints a success message.

4. Running the Script:

Save the script as a Python file (e.g., rename_images.py). Open a terminal, navigate to the listing containing the script and your files, and execute it using the Python command:

Bash
python rename_images.py
Use code with caution.

This will run the script and rename your picture documents according to your specifications.

Expanding Your Automation Arsenal: Exploring More Possibilities

The probabilities for automation with Python scripts are vast. Here are some additional examples:

Web Scraping: Extract data from websites and organize it into a structured format.

Data Cleaning and Formatting: Automate repetitive duties like casting off duplicates, correcting inconsistencies, and formatting facts in spreadsheets.

File Organization: Move, copy, sort, and rename files based totally on specific criteria.

Social Media Management: Schedule posts, reply to comments, and generate reports.

Email Automation: Send personalized emails or automatic notifications based totally on events.

By leveraging Python's competencies and exploring more than a few libraries for file handling, internet interaction, and statistics manipulation, you can automate a huge variety of duties and notably beautify your productivity

Chapter 17: Beyond the Basics: Where to Go Next in Your Python Journey (Web Development, Machine Learning, and More!)

Congratulations! You've successfully navigated the fundamentals of Python programming and unlocked its viability for several tasks is simply the start of your exciting Python adventure. This chapter explores some of the most popular and rewarding paths you can pursue to in addition make your Python expertise.

Web Development: Building Interactive Applications

The web is an enormous landscape, and Python performs a necessary function in its development. Here are some interesting web improvement avenues you can explore with Python:

Full-Stack Development: Utilize frameworks like Django or Flask to build both the backend (server-side) logic and frontend (user interface) of internet applications. Django is regarded for its complete structure and safety features, whilst Flask provides extra flexibility for smaller projects.

Web Scraping: Extract statistics from websites on the usage of libraries like Beautiful Soup or Scrapy. These records can be used for several purposes, such as market research, fee comparison, or constructing data-driven applications.

Web APIs: Develop APIs (Application Programming Interfaces) that enable different functions to access and engage with your data or functionality with the use of Python frameworks like Django REST framework or FastAPI.

Here are some assets to get you began with web improvement in the usage of Python:

Django Tutorial: https://docs.djangoproject.com/en/5.0/intro/

Flask Tutorial: https://blog.miguelgrinberg.com/post/the-flask-mega-tutorial-part-i-hello-world

Beautiful Soup Documentation: https://www.crummy.com/software/BeautifulSoup/??

Scrapy Documentation: https://doc.scrapy.org/

Data Science and Machine Learning: Unveiling Insights from Data
The world is brimming with data, and Python is a powerhouse for extracting know-how and insights from it. Here's how you can delve into the exciting realms of statistics science and machine learning:

Data Analysis: Libraries like Pandas and NumPy grant effective tools for facts wrangling, cleaning, manipulation, and statistical analysis.
Machine Learning: Frameworks like sci-kit-learn offer a wealthy set of

algorithms for tasks like classification, regression, clustering, and more. You can instruct these algorithms on labeled datasets to research patterns and make predictions on new, unseen data.

Deep Learning: Libraries like TensorFlow and PyTorch allow you to build and teach complex neural networks for tasks like image recognition, natural language processing, and recommender systems.

Here are some resources to kickstart your information science and desktop getting-to-know trip with Python:

Pandas Tutorial: https://pandas.pydata.org/docs/

NumPy Tutorial: https://numpy.org/doc/

Scikit-learn Tutorial: https://scikit-learn.org/
TensorFlow Tutorials: https://www.tensorflow.org/tutorials
PyTorch Tutorials: https://pytorch.org/tutorials/

Scientific Computing and Automation: Python Beyond Web and Data

Python's versatility extends past web development and facts science. Here are some charming areas the place you can leverage its power:

Scientific Computing: Libraries like SciPy and Matplotlib furnish superior mathematical functions, statistics visualization tools, and functionalities for solving complex scientific problems.

Automation: As explored in Chapter 16, Python excels at automating repetitive tasks on your computer. You can use libraries like os and subprocess to engage with the operating system, control documents, and directories, and automate a range of workflows.

Game Development: With libraries like Pygame, you can create engaging 2D games, while frameworks like PyOpenGL allow you to challenge the realm of 3D recreation development.

Here are some assets to explore Python for scientific computing and automation:

- **SciPy Documentation:** https://docs.scipy.org/doc/scipy/

- **Matplotlib Tutorial:**
  https://matplotlib.org/stable/tutorials/index.html
- **Pygame Tutorial:**
  https://www.pygame.org/wiki/tutorials
- **PyOpenGL Tutorial:**
  https://pyopengl.sourceforge.net/documentation/index.html

Choosing Your Path: Consider Your Interests and Goals

The substantial world of Python provides a multitude of paths to explore. When determining where to go next, reflect on your interests, professional aspirations, and the kinds of troubles you'd like to solve. Here are some additional tips:

Experiment with special libraries and frameworks: The pleasant way to find out what excites you is to try things out. Most libraries offer beginner-friendly tutorials and projects to get you started.

Build small projects: Solidify your gaining knowledge via building non-public initiatives that observe your newly obtained skills. Start with smaller tasks and gradually expand complexity as you acquire experience.

Engage with the Python community: Numerous online forums, communities, and meetups cater to Python programmers of all levels.

Sources
info

1. github.com/schererjulie/CodingTempleBootcamp
2. github.com/SLongofono/448_Project1

Bonus Chapter: Python in 2024 and Beyond - Exploring the Future of the Language

Python has established itself as a dominant force in the programming world, valued for its readability, versatility, and significant ecosystem of libraries. As we appear toward 2024 and beyond, various exciting trends are shaping the future of Python and its manageable applications.

The Rise of Full-Stack Python: Simplifying Web Development

Full-stack frameworks like Django and Flask are anticipated to continue evolving, presenting streamlined development workflows for building both backend (server-side) and frontend (user interface) components of internet functions with Python.

Integration with frontend frameworks like React and Vue.js will probably come even smoother, permitting developers to leverage the strengths of each Python for backend common sense and famous JavaScript frameworks for interactive consumer interfaces.

Backend-as-a-service (BaaS) structures built with Python might gain traction, providing pre-built functionalities for common web development duties like consumer authentication, database management, and file storage, further simplifying the procedure for developers.

AI and Machine Learning: Python as the Language of Choice

The popularity of Python for machine getting-to-know and artificial intelligence (AI) improvement is probable to soar. Its clear syntax, huge libraries like TensorFlow and PyTorch, and growing ecosystem of AI-focused equipment will solidify its function as the go-to language for building sensible systems.

AutoML (Automated Machine Learning) libraries that automate duties like hyperparameter tuning and model choice are predicted to end up greater sophisticated, making desktop getting-to-know reachable to a wider range of developers, even those bearing a robust heritage in AI.

Explainable AI (XAI) techniques are likely to become increasingly necessary as rules and ethical issues around AI adoption grow. Python libraries that assist developers in apprehending and interpreting the decision-making tactics of their computer gaining knowledge of fashions will be in high demand.

The Power of Data Science: Python at the Forefront

Data science workflows will probably become extra streamlined with the integration of cloud-based systems and huge records processing tools written in Python.

Data visualization libraries like Matplotlib and Seaborn will proceed to evolve, providing more superior aspects for creating interactive and informative visualizations that effectively talk insights from data analysis.

The rise of domain-specific languages (DSLs) built on top of Python is a potential trend. These DSLs would furnish an extra concise and intuitive way to specific information evaluation tasks specific to certain domains like finance, biology, or social sciences.

Focus on Security and Efficiency

Security issues in Python development will emerge as

paramount. Libraries and frameworks are probably to prioritize security features, and satisfactory practices for secure coding in Python will be broadly emphasized.

Performance optimization methods will grow to be extra vital as Python is used for more and more complex statistics processing and computationally intensive tasks. Libraries like NumPy might see similar optimizations, and tools for profiling and optimizing Python code will obtain more prominence.

The Expanding Ecosystem: Embracing New Technologies

Integration with rising applied sciences like blockchain and the

Internet of Things (IoT) will probably see an upward thrust in Python-based solutions. Frameworks and libraries specially designed for interacting with blockchain networks or creating IoT purposes using Python are predicted to emerge.

Quantum computing, although nevertheless in its early stages, has the attainability to revolutionize quite several fields. Python libraries and tools that facilitate the improvement of quantum algorithms and applications will possibly grow to be a fact in the not-so-distant future.

This glimpse into the future of Python highlights its non-stop evolution and adaptation to meet the ever-changing demands of the tech landscape. By embracing these trends and actively engaging with the Python community, builders can make sure they are well-equipped to leverage the energy of this versatile language for years to come.

Appendix: Resources Galore - A Cheat Sheet for Your Coding Adventures

Congratulations on embarking on your Python programming journey! This appendix serves as your one-stop keep for a multitude of assets to beautify your studying and exploration of the Python world.

Official Python Documentation: The Ultimate Guide

The respectable Python documentation is a beneficial resource for the entirety of Python-related. It covers all components of the language, from basic syntax and facts sorts to superior facets and modules. Here's the link to get you started:

Python Documentation: https://www.python.org/doc/

This complete documentation presents distinctive explanations, code examples, and references to the core Python language. Dive into precise subjects like:

Language Fundamentals: Learn about variables, facts types, operators, manipulate flow statements, functions, and more.

The Standard Library: Explore the widespread collection of built-in modules and features that come with Python, overlaying several functionalities like file handling, networking, and data manipulation.

Advanced Topics: Delve into deeper concepts like object-oriented programming, exception handling, metaprogramming, and working with external libraries.

Reliable documentation is a dependable supply of truth and needs to be your important reference point every time you have a question about Python syntax, functionality, or nice practices.

Online Courses and Tutorials: Interactive Learning at Your Pace

There's a wealth of online publications and tutorials on hand for Python beginners of all levels. Here are some popular systems to consider:

Coursera: https://www.coursera.org/ offers a range of Python courses from pinnacle universities and companies, ranging from novice introductions to advanced specializations.

edX: https://www.edx.org/ offers comparable path constructions to Coursera, with a focal point on interactive knowledge of and hands-on exercises.

Udacity: https://www.udacity.com/ offers project-oriented nano degrees that combine video lectures, quizzes, and real-world initiatives to solidify your Python skills.

DataCamp: https://www.datacamp.com/ specializes in facts science and machine studying courses, instructing Python within the context of records evaluation and visualization.

Codecademy: https://www.codecademy.com/ gives interactive coding challenges and projects that introduce you to Python standards in a gamified way.

These platforms furnish structured studying paths, video lectures, coding exercises, and quizzes to help you study Python at your own pace. Many courses offer certificates upon completion, which can be precious additions to your expert portfolio.

Books: In-Depth Exploration for Dedicated Learners

For those who decide on a more typical getting-to-know style, numerous Python books cater to all ride levels. Here are some broadly endorsed options:

Automate the Boring Stuff with Python by way of Al Sweigart: A gentle introduction to Python, perfect for beginners with no prior programming experience. It focuses on realistic functions of Python for automating everyday tasks.

Fluent Python by Luciano Ramalho: Aimed at intermediate Python programmers, this e-book delves deeper into core Python concepts, idioms, and quality practices, supporting you to write clean, efficient, and Pythonic code.

Python Crash Course via Eric Matthes: A project-based introduction to Python, especially well-suited for those interested in mastering Python for game development.

Data Science for Business through Foster Provost and Tom Fawcett: If you are involved in statistics science, this e-book makes use of Python to introduce vital data analysis ideas and techniques.